A TRUE BOOK™

The New Jersey Colony

KEVIN CUNNINGHAM

Children's Press®
An Imprint of Scholastic Inc.
New York   Toronto   London   Auckland   Sydney
Mexico City   New Delhi   Hong Kong
Danbury, Connecticut

Content Consultant
Jeffrey Kaja, PhD
Associate Professor of History
California State University, Northridge

Library of Congress Cataloging-in-Publication Data

Cunningham, Kevin, 1966–
  The New Jersey Colony/Kevin Cunningham.
      p. cm.—(A true book)
  Includes bibliographical references and index.
  ISBN-13: 978-0-531-25393-9 (lib. bdg.)   ISBN-13: 978-0-531-26606-9 (pbk.)
  ISBN-10: 0-531-25393-9 (lib. bdg.)   ISBN-10: 0-531-26606-9 (pbk.)
  1. New Jersey—History—Colonial period, ca. 1600–1775—Juvenile
literature. 2. New Jersey—History—Revolution, 1775–1783—Juvenile
literature. I. Title. II. Series.
  F137.C95 2012
  974.9'02—dc22   2011010221

All rights reserved. Published in 2012 by Children's Press, an imprint of Scholastic Inc.
Printed in China 62
SCHOLASTIC, CHILDREN'S PRESS, A TRUE BOOK, and associated logos are trademarks and/or registered trademarks of Scholastic Inc.
1 2 3 4 5 6 7 8 9 10 R 21 20 19 18 17 16 15 14 13 12

Find the Truth!

Everything you are about to read is true *except* for one of the sentences on this page.

Which one is **TRUE**?

T or F Farm owners in New Jersey never used slave labor.

T or F Quaker women had more freedoms than women in other religious groups.

Find the answers in this book.

3

Timeline of New Jersey Colony History

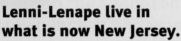

1500s

Lenni-Lenape live in what is now New Jersey.

1609

Henry Hudson explores the region of New Jersey.

1777

The Continental army wins the Battle of Princeton.

1787

New Jersey approves the U.S. Constitution.

CHAPTER 1

The Native Americans

The region that we now call New Jersey was home to the Lenni-Lenape people in the 1500s. These Native Americans lived in clans of related families. Their villages included domed wigwams and longhouses shaped like loaves of bread. They constructed both kinds of buildings by placing mats of tree bark, grass, and animal skins over a wooden frame. A hole in the ceiling allowed smoke from their cooking fires to escape.

The Lenni-Lenape Diet

Lenni-Lenape depended on crops such as maize (corn), beans, and squash. Women planted and farmed the clan's fields. They also kept gardens and gathered wild foods such as berries and onions. Men hunted deer and other game with bows and short spears. Many Lenni-Lenape moved to the seashore during summers. Men netted and speared fish and turtles. Women collected other seafood such as clams and oysters.

Food such as corn could be stored for later use.

A clan's women controlled its property.

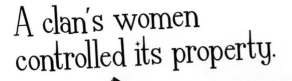

Bones were often used as knife handles.

The Lenni-Lenape didn't know how to make metal tools. They crafted drill-like tools from bone and antler. They made arrowheads from bone and rock. They also made scraping and slicing tools from seashells. Deerskin and furs provided much of their clothing and bedding. Lenni-Lenape woodworkers made everything from bowls to canoes. A desire for new tools would eventually affect their relationship with Europeans settlers.

NEW YORK

Hudson River

Area enlarged

Original 13 Colonies

Delaware River

Kittatinny Mountains

• Franklin

Hackensack •

Morristown •

Bergen •

New Amsterdam (New York)

LENNI-LENAPE

Perth Amboy •

New Brunswick •

PENNSYLVANIA

• Princeton

Shrewsbury •

• Trenton

Delaware River

• Burlington

Philadelphia • • Glouster

NEW JERSEY

Colonial boundaries
Present boundaries

MARYLAND

DELAWARE

□ Salem
Fort Elfsborg

• Mays Landing

Delaware Bay

Cape May

ATLANTIC OCEAN

0   miles   20
0   km   20

CHAPTER 2

A New Colony

The Lenni-Lenape first encountered Europeans when Italian explorer Giovanni da Verrazzano landed in the region in 1524. Permanent contact began in 1609 when Henry Hudson claimed a huge part of the Lenni-Lenape lands for the Netherlands. A Dutch company called the Dutch West India Company built trading posts along the Delaware River in the 1620s. The Lenni-Lenape provided Dutch traders with beaver furs. The furs were made into expensive hats and coats in Europe.

The fur trade was an important part of the relationship between the natives and the early European settlers.

The Dutch traded items such as metal pots, cloth, and guns to the Native Americans in return. The Dutch West India Company soon created a colony called New Netherland to take advantage of the fur trade. But fur traders usually made their money and returned to Europe. The company wanted people to settle in New Netherland for good. Only a few took the offer, even when it included free land.

Taxes, Trouble, and Trade

The company sent Willem Kieft to lead New Netherland in 1639. Kieft risked harming the fur trade by ordering the Lenni-Lenape to pay taxes. They refused. The two sides began to fight. A Lenni-Lenape man took revenge on a colonist. Kieft then led a bloody attack that killed dozens of villagers. A war followed. Hundreds of people in the Hudson River area died. The war almost destroyed New Netherland.

Kieft's leadership resulted in a violent feud with the Lenni-Lenape.

After being fired for his poor leadership, Kieft died on the way back to the Netherlands.

New company governor Peter Stuyvesant rebuilt the colony. But new problems arose by 1651. The fur trade had attracted people from many European countries. They competed with one another for furs. A small Swedish colony called New Sweden claimed land around the Delaware River in 1638. Dutch soldiers took control of New Sweden. They hoped to keep it from competing in the fur trade with New Netherland.

Many Swedish settlers began arriving in the 1630s.

Part of New Netherland later became New York state.

Slave Labor

Farming played a growing role in New Netherland. But the colony had problems convincing settlers to cross the Atlantic Ocean to work the farms.

Slavery quickly became an important part of the colonial economy.

New Netherland began to use enslaved Africans as workers. Large farms had the most slaves. But some small farm owners also used slave labor. About one-tenth of New Netherlands population was made up of enslaved people by the 1660s.

George Carteret helped to develop New Jersey into an English colony.

Carteret also helped to found the Carolina colonies.

A Change in Leadership

The Dutch faced pressure from a powerful competitor. England had colonies up and down the Atlantic Coast. English warships and soldiers took New Amsterdam without a fight in 1664. New Netherland became New York. King Charles II of England gave Dutch lands south of the Hudson River to George Carteret and John Berkeley. Carteret named the area New Jersey, after the area where he lived in England.

Carteret and Berkeley attracted new settlers by promising religious freedom to all New Jersey colonists. Religious groups such as the **Quakers** and Puritans flocked to northern New Jersey to start farms. The Lenni-Lenape began to suffer from diseases the Europeans had brought with them. The numbers of Lenni-Lenape were reduced from thousands to hundreds. Many sold their land to settlers. Others moved west to Ohio and Pennsylvania.

Quaker and Puritan farms began to appear throughout the colony.

New Freedoms

Berkeley sold his part of New Jersey to Quakers. The colony split between Quaker West Jersey and Carteret's East Jersey in 1676. The Quakers wrote a **constitution** guaranteeing its settlers many rights. It included the right to vote for local government officials. The two Jerseys rejoined in 1702 when the English government took control of New Jersey away from the private owners. About 10,000 people lived in New Jersey by the next year.

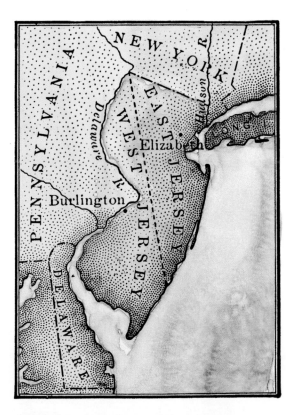

New Jersey was split almost exactly down the middle toward the end of the 17th century.

Farming had replaced fur trading as New Jersey's major occupation. Colonists made Native American foods such as maize and beans a part of their diet. Bread products were made from wheat and oats. Wheat also became a **cash crop**. It was sold to Europe and the Caribbean. A typical New Jersey village had at least one mill. Waterpower was used at mills to grind wheat and other grains into flour.

Mills were an important tool for grain farmers.

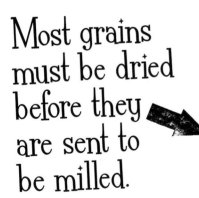

Most grains must be dried before they are sent to be milled.

Colonial women were responsible for many household chores.

CHAPTER 3

Everyday Life

Colonial women often married young and raised large families. They cooked and took care of their young children. Women kept gardens and spun thread and yarn. They also mended clothes and preserved food. Some women crafted items such as soap and candles to sell for extra money. Sybilla Masters was born in Burlington, New Jersey. She invented a new device to clean corn. She was the first American woman to earn a **patent**.

← A woman's property belonged to her husband once she married.

The Quakers were one of the only religions to allow women any rights.

Quakers, also known as Friends, remain active today.

Lack of Rights

Colonial society taught a woman to obey her husband. English law prevented married women from owning property. Only widowed women could do so. Women could not hold patents. This meant Sybilla Masters had to patent her invention in her husband's name. But Quaker women had more opportunities than elsewhere in the colonies. Some women even became Quaker ministers. These tolerant attitudes made the Quakers unpopular with other religious groups.

Elizabeth Haddon Estaugh

John Haddon bought land in New Jersey in 1698 with the hope of practicing his Quaker faith there. Poor health kept him from leaving England.

His 21-year-old daughter Elizabeth went instead. She married a minister-physician named John Estaugh after arriving in West Jersey. She and her husband soon founded the town of Haddonfield. Elizabeth managed the land in her own name after John died.

Children often helped with the chores on family farms.

Out in the Fields

Most men in New Jersey owned or worked on farms. The average colony farm was about 200 acres (81 hectares). But some families had only enough land to provide for their most basic needs. Colonial farmers lacked machines. Animals and the families' own muscles provided power. Oxen pulled plows. Men planted crops and built fences. They harvested wheat and other crops with hand tools. Farmers often worked from sunrise to sunset.

Potters used a special glaze on their dishes that prevented liquids from soaking into the pottery.

It took several years for an apprentice to learn the skills of a trade.

Other Jobs

New Jersey had about 60 towns by the mid-1700s. Trained tradesmen worked as barrel makers, carpenters, and millers in these towns. Many tradesmen taught their skills to **apprentices**. Apprentices worked for five to six years. They then left to get jobs of their own. New Jersey manufactured pottery for sale in the colonies. The forests provided wood for shipbuilding. Miners dug up iron used to make kettles and cannonballs.

Growing Up

Not all children in the colony went to school. Those who did had to finish a long list of chores before heading off to spend a few hours at the schoolhouse. Children of all ages sat in a single classroom. Teachers punished misbehavior by spanking or smacking children's knuckles with a wooden rod. Children learned basic subjects such as reading, writing, and math. Only a small number of children received more education. These children were usually boys.

Most colonial schoolhouses had just a single classroom.

In 2008, New Jersey became the first northern state to officially apologize for its role in allowing slavery in the United States.

Charlestown, July 24th, 1769.

TO BE SOLD,

On THURSDAY the third Day of AUGUST next,

A CARGO OF NINETY-FOUR PRIME, HEALTHY

NEGROES,

CONSISTING OF

Thirty-nine MEN, Fifteen BOYS, Twenty-four WOMEN, and Sixteen GIRLS.

JUST ARRIVED,

In the Brigantine DEMBIA, Francis Bare, Master, from SIERRA-LEON, by

DAVID & JOHN DEAS.

There were more than 13,000 slaves living in New Jersey by the early 1800s.

Life as a Slave

Slavery was not as important to the economy of New Jersey as it was to the southern states. Enslaved people in New Jersey had some rights. It was not unusual for them to live in the same house as their masters. Yet enslaved people were still considered the property of their owners. Many of them escaped into New Jersey's thick forests and swamps.

Not all farmers owned or had permission to use the land they farmed.

CHAPTER 4

The Road to Independence

New Jersey had the best system of roads in the American colonies. Ferries brought goods across rivers for sale in New York and Philadelphia. This added to the colony's prosperity. But not everyone shared in the colony's success. Poor farmers and squatters clashed with the leaders of West Jersey. Squatters were newcomers who farmed open land without buying it. Groups attacked jails to free farmers and squatters. Riots broke out in many small towns.

Only about 25 percent of New Jersey's colonial land titles were officially recorded.

The governor took sides against the poorer farmers and squatters. The king of England chose the governor. The protesters blamed him as well as officials in the colonies. Anti-British feelings grew in the 1720s and 1730s. A religious movement called the Great Awakening spread through the colonies at that time. The ideas it introduced about religious and human freedom inspired many religions to become more **democratic**. These ideas soon spread to other areas of society.

The Great Awakening was led by preachers such as George Whitefield.

A second Great Awakening occurred in the early 19th century.

The colonists were not happy to learn about the Stamp Act.

Paying for Victory

Britain signed a peace treaty with France for control of North America in 1763. The war had been expensive for Britain. It needed to raise money to pay off war debt. Parliament, the British **legislature**, chose to raise money by taxing the American colonies. A tax on sugar and other products was passed in Parliament in 1764.

The Stamp Act of 1765 forced colonists to buy a British stamp to put on paper materials such as newspapers and playing cards.

People protested the Stamp Act throughout the colonies.

Taxation Without Representation

Colonists argued that taxes should not be placed on them because the colonies had no representatives in Parliament to speak for their rights. Colonists called it "taxation without representation." But they were not against all taxes.

Taxes paid to the colony were acceptable because colonists elected representatives to New Jersey's legislature. Protests and a **boycott** against British goods eventually convinced Parliament to end the Stamp Act in early 1766.

The destruction of the tea became known as the Boston Tea Party.

Patriots dressed as American Indians before boarding the tea ship.

New taxes were passed and then canceled. But a tax on tea remained. This caused anti-British feeling to grow throughout the colonies. Britain's government added to the problem by allowing a British company to sell its tea tax-free. American companies still had to pay the tax. **Patriots** protested by tossing British tea into Boston Harbor in December 1773. Britain closed the harbor. Parliament limited Massachusetts' control of its own government.

First Continental Congress

Representatives from 12 colonies met at the First Continental Congress in Philadelphia in 1774. They discussed the unfair treatment by Parliament, boycotting English goods and sending a letter to King George III. Protests and boycotts continued. Patriots in Greenwich, New Jersey, burned stolen British tea in the town square in December 1774. British troops and Massachusetts **militia** clashed west of Boston the following April. The American Revolutionary War had begun.

Georgia was the only colony not to send a representative to the Continental Congress.

Fifty-six men participated in the First Continental Congress.

The winter of 1776 marked an important turning point in the war.

Battle in New Jersey

New Jersey soon became an important battleground in the war. The British almost destroyed George Washington's Continental army outside New York City in September 1776. Washington retreated across the river to New Jersey. He called upon the local militia for help. But no one responded. The Continentals fled to Pennsylvania while the British invaded New Jersey. Winter settled in. Patriot hopes were fading. Washington looked for a chance to strike back.

New Jersey's Founding Fathers

New Jersey held its own congressional meeting in May 1775. The representatives made a point of stating their loyalty to King George III. But by May 1776, a new congress supported breaking away from Britain. A Second Continental Congress with representatives from across the colonies had also begun to favor independence. After much discussion, the representatives voted for the Declaration of Independence on July 2. Five New Jersey representatives signed the declaration. Three are pictured here.

John Hart

"Honest John" Hart was a successful farmer elected to the Second Continental Congress. He hid in the Sourland Mountains after British troops invaded New Jersey. Hart invited Washington and 12,000 Continental soldiers to camp on his land prior to the Battle of Monmouth.

Richard Stockton

Richard Stockton was captured at a friend's New Jersey home after serving with the Continental army in late 1776. The British put him in irons, starved him, and kept him in freezing cold weather. He was exchanged for British prisoners six weeks later. But the time in prison ruined his health.

John Witherspoon

John Witherspoon was born in Scotland. He was president of what became Princeton University. He played major roles in the Second Continental Congress and the effort to approve the U.S. Constitution. He used his own money to help rebuild the university after the war.

Surprise Attack

Armies in the 1700s usually stopped fighting during wintertime. Washington planned to surprise the British with an attack on Trenton, New Jersey. He led his men through a snowstorm and captured 900 of Britain's German allies on Christmas night 1776. The Continentals then beat British forces at Princeton on January 3, 1777. British troops pulled out of all but one corner of New Jersey. Washington had given the colonists hope again.

Washington's forces scored major victories at Trenton and Princeton.

Washington's army numbered about 6,000 at the beginning of 1777.

About one-third of all colonists remained loyal to Great Britain during the revolution.

Battle of Monmouth

The Continentals caught British troops marching from Philadelphia to New York on June 28, 1778. The battle raged back and forth. It ended in a draw. But it showed for the first time that the Continental army was the fighting equal of its British enemies. Patriot and **Loyalist** neighbors also battled one another. Patriots looted Loyalist houses and hanged suspected Loyalists. Loyalists burned Patriot homes and murdered militiamen.

William Livingston

William Livingston was a lawyer and one-time newspaper owner. He replaced William Franklin, the Loyalist son of Patriot Benjamin Franklin, as governor of New Jersey in 1776. Livingston had served in the Continental Congress and the militia. He led and helped train troops as a Continental general during the Revolutionary War. His family spent the war in the safety of Parsippany, New Jersey. He continued as governor after the war and signed the U.S. Constitution.

After the War

The British surrendered to American forces in 1781 after their defeat at Yorktown. New Jersey was free. But the war had destroyed large parts of the state. Wagons and soldiers' boots had chewed up valuable farmland. Towns lay in ruins. Soldiers on both sides had robbed and burned homes. Thousands of Loyalists and slaves had fled with the British. William Livingston led the state in the slow work of rebuilding.

With the war over, the people of the United States set about rebuilding their nation.

Around 100,000 Loyalists left the country after the war.

Voting on the Constitution

The new nation faced a decision about whether to create a strong national government overseeing all the states. Representatives from 12 states met in Philadelphia in 1787 to write a new U.S. Constitution. The document would create a national government. But it would also include limits on its powers. The Constitution went to each state to be voted on. New Jersey voted to accept it and became the young nation's third state. ★

The U.S. Constitution marked the beginning of the country as we know it today.

There were 55 representatives at the Constitutional Convention.

True Statistics

Year Henry Hudson visited the New Jersey area: 1609

Number of colonists in New Jersey in 1703: About 10,000

Average farm size in 1740s: About 200 acres (81 ha)

Weight of the smallest cannonball: 2 lbs. (0.9 kg)

Number of New Jersey colonists who signed the Declaration of Independence: 5

Number of enemy troops captured at the Battle of Trenton: 900

Number of winters George Washington spent in New Jersey: 3

Number of New Jersey men serving in the Continental army: About 4,000

Population of New Jersey in 1783: 180,000

Did you find the truth?

(F) Farm owners in New Jersey never used slave labor.

(T) Quaker women had more freedoms than women in other religious groups.

Resources

Books

Downey, Tika. *New Jersey the Garden State*. New York: PowerKids, 2010.

Dubois, Muriel L. *The New Jersey Colony*. Mankato, MN: Capstone, 2006.

Englar, Mary. *Dutch Colonies in America*. Mankato, MN: Compass Point, 2009.

Gibson, Karen B. *New Netherland: The Dutch Settle the Hudson Valley*. Hockessin, DE: Mitchell Lane, 2006.

Heinrichs, Ann. *New Jersey*. Mankato, MN: Compass Point, 2003.

Murphy, Jim. *The Crossing: How George Washington Saved the American Revolution*. New York: Scholastic, 2010.

Scholl, Elizabeth J. *New Jersey*. New York: Children's Press, 2008.

Stewart, Mark. *New Jersey Native Peoples*. Chicago: Heinemann Library, 2004.

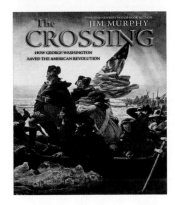

Organizations and Web Sites

Delaware (Lenni-Lenape) Nation

www.delawarenation.com
Study the history of New Jersey's Native American peoples and learn what is happening in the Delaware/Lenni-Lenape Nation today.

New Jersey Historical Society

www.jerseyhistory.org
See articles and photographs on various parts of state history, and get advice on doing research projects.

Places to Visit

New Jersey State Museum

205 West State Street
Trenton, NJ 08625
(609) 292-6464
www.state.nj.us/state/museum/index.htm
Study exhibits that take you through the history of New Jersey from prehistory to the present.

Old Barracks Museum

Barrack Street
Trenton, NJ 08608
(609) 396-1776
www.barracks.org
Visit a living museum of a barracks built in the French and Indian War and later used by Continental army troops after the Battle of Trenton in 1776.

Important Words

apprentices (uh-PREN-ti-sez)—people who learn a skill by working with an expert

boycott (BOI-kaht)—refusing to buy goods from a person, group, or country

cash crop (KASH KRAHP)—a crop grown for sale rather than for a family's own use

constitution (kahn-sti-TOO-shuhn)—the laws of a country that state the rights of the people and the powers of government

democratic (dem-uh-KRAT-ik)—a system of electing leaders by the votes of citizens

legislature (LEJ-is-lay-chur)—a group of people who have the power to make or change laws

Loyalist (LOI-uhl-ist)—an American colonist who remained faithful to Great Britain

militia (muh-LISH-uh)—a group of people who are trained to fight but who aren't professional soldiers

patent (PAT-uhnt)—a document that gives an inventor the right to make or profit from an invention

Patriots (PAY-tree-uhts)—American colonists opposed to Great Britain

Quakers (KWAY-kurz)—the Society of Friends, a religious group that believes in equality and nonviolence

Index

Page numbers in **bold** indicate illustrations

Battle of Monmouth, 37, 39
Battle of Princeton, 6, **38**
Battle of Trenton, **38**
Berkeley, John, 16, 17, 18
Boston Tea Party, **33**

Carteret, George, **16**–17, 18
Charles II, king of England, 16
children, 21, **24**, **26**
constitutions, **6**, 18, 37, 40, **42**
Constitutional Convention, **42**
Continental army, **35**, 37, **38**, 39, 40
Continental Congress, **34**, **36**, 37, 40

Declaration of Independence, 36
Delaware River, 11, 14
Dutch West India Company, 11, 12, 13, 14

East Jersey, **18**
education, **26**
Estaugh, Elizabeth Haddon, 23
European exploration, **6**, 11

foods, **8**, 19, 21
fur trade, 11–**12**, 13, 14, 19

George III, king of England, 34, 36
governors, **13**, 14, 30, **40**
Great Awakening, **30**
Great Britain, 16, 18, 22, 30, 31, 32, 33, 34, 35, 36, 37, 38, **39**, 41

Haddonfield, **23**
Haddon, John, 23
houses, 7, **17**, **20**, 27, **28**, **39**, 41
Hudson, Henry, **6**, 11

legislature, 31, 32, 33, 34

Livingston, William, **40**, 41
Loyalists, **39**, 40, 41

maps, **10**, **18**
Masters, Sybilla, 21, 22
militias, 34, 35, 39, 40
mills, **19**, 25

Native Americans, **6**, 7, 8–**9**, 11–**12**, 13, 17, 19
New Amsterdam, 16
New Netherland colony, 12, 13, 14, **15**, 16
New Sweden colony, **14**

Parliament, 31, 32, 33, 34
Patriots, **33**, 34, 35, **39**, 40
protests, 30, **32**, 33, 34
Puritans, **17**

Quakers, **17**, 18, **22**, 23

religious beliefs, **17**, 18, **22**, 23, **30**
Revolutionary War, **6**, 34, **35**, 37, **38**, **39**, 40

slavery, **15**, **27**, 41
Stamp Act (1765), **31**, **32**
statehood, 42

taxes, 13, **31**, **32**–33
tea, **33**, 34

U.S. Constitution, **6**, 37, 40, **42**

Washington, George, 35, 37, **38**
West Jersey, **18**, 23, 29
wigwams, 7
women, 8, 9, **20**, 21, **22**

About the Author

Kevin Cunningham has written more than 40 books on disasters, the history of disease, Native Americans, and other topics. Cunningham lives near Chicago with his wife and young daughter.